Disney · PIXAR
FINDING DORY

An Ocean Full of Friends

Disney · PIXAR
FINDING
DORY

An Ocean Full of Friends

By Barbara Bazaldua

INCREDI
BUILDS™

A Division of Insight Editions, LP
San Rafael, California

Anemone where Marlin and Nemo live sting-free

Dory's cozy home close to Marlin and Nemo.

Home Sweet Reef

DORY

Since the previous year, when Dory helped Marlin find his son, Nemo, the friendly and vivacious blue tang had lived happily with them in the coral reef.

But when Dory accompanied Nemo's class on a field trip to watch a stingray migration, she suddenly remembered something she had forgotten. She has a family. She just couldn't remember their names . . . or where they were. . . .

The Drop Off is this way.

AMAZING CORAL REEFS

- The coral that makes up reefs aren't plants—they're tiny animals.

- Corals are ancient animals related to jellyfish and anemones.

- The largest coral reef in the world is the Great Barrier Reef in Australia. It's more than 1,200 miles (1,900 kilometers) long.

- Thousands of marine species live in coral reefs.

> "I remember it like it was yesterday. Of course, I don't really remember yesterday all that well."

WHERE'S MY FAMILY?

All Dory could remember about her family and where they might be were the words, "Jewel of Morro Bay, California."

It wasn't much information, but Dory had to start somewhere, and she was determined to go.

"I'm Dory. I've lost my family. Can you help me?"

BABY DORY

FRIENDLY BUT FORGETFUL

Upbeat, optimistic Dory has an amazing ability to make friends with everyone she meets. Over . . . and over . . . and over. That's because she has short-term memory loss and quickly forgets that she's just met someone. The plucky blue tang doesn't get discouraged, though. Her motto has always been: "Just keep swimming; just keep swimming."

When she was young, Dory loved looking for shells with her mom. One day, Dory saw a beautiful purple shell. Her mom would love it! So Dory darted over to retrieve it. Suddenly an undertow pulled Dory deep into the ocean. She was lost. Worst of all, she couldn't remember where she was from or who her parents were. Although other fish saw her swimming alone and asked if they could help her, Dory couldn't even remember what she was looking for. Poor Dory! For a long time, she was all alone in the ocean. It wasn't until Dory met Marlin and joined his search for his son, Nemo, that Dory found loyal, caring friends who would stick by her. Uh . . . what were their names again?

A Loving Family

"We will never forget you, Dory. And we know you'll never forget us."

"See, Kelpcake. There's always another way!"

JENNY

Cheerful, loving Jenny may seem a bit scatterbrained, but she is actually very wise—especially about her daughter Dory and what she needs. Jenny was determined to help Dory learn the skills she needed to get along despite her less-than-perfect memory. And when Dory was lost, Jenny was sure that someday, somehow, she would return.

CHARLIE

Dory's dad, Charlie, loves to joke around, but he never kids about his family. He adores Jenny and doted on Dory, doing everything he could think of to teach his daughter how to survive. Like Jenny, Charlie never gave up hope that someday Dory would remember them and return.

TERRIFIC BLUE TANG FACTS

- Blue tangs are yellow when they're young and turn blue as they mature.
- Sharp spines on their tails (called tangs) help protect blue tangs from predators.
- Blue tangs can change the intensity of their color.
- Algae for dinner? Yum! It's what blue tangs love to eat.

Dory's Best Friends

NEMO

Determined to search for her family, Dory asked Marlin and Nemo to go with her to California.

At first, Marlin didn't want to go. He had had enough traveling, he told Dory, and he had serious doubts about the wisdom of trying to swim across such an enormous ocean. But Marlin also understood what it was like to lose family, so at last he agreed to the journey. He even suggested a great way to travel.

MARLIN

He may be a clownfish, but Marlin isn't exactly a bundle of laughs. In fact, he's a bit of a worrier and a pessimist. A homebody, Marlin was perfectly happy staying in his snug anemone. Another journey—no thank you! But, in the end, his loyalty and kindness won out, and he agreed to go with Dory and Nemo. It took a lot of courage for Marlin to break out of his ordinary routine but, once again, he proved that he has more courage in his little fin than many bigger fish.

NEMO

Happy-go-lucky Nemo is just a normal kid clownfish. He likes going to school and hanging out with his friends on the reef. But when Dory asked for help, Nemo was willing to leave the safety of the reef. His earlier adventures had boosted his self-confidence. Besides, he understands how it feels to be separated from family, and what it's like to be different. So he was ready to dive in and help Dory however he could.

CURIOUS CLOWNFISH FACTS

- Clownfish scales have a mucous coating that protects them from anemone stings.

- Before moving into an anemone, clownfish perform an elaborate dance touching all the parts of their bodies to the anemone's tentacles.

- Clownfish are also called anemonefish.

- Anemones protect clownfish from predators. In return, clownfish bring anemones food and keep their tentacles clean.

"It's the California Current, dude. Got some gnarly chop! Surf's up, dude!"

CRUSH

CRUISING THE CURRENT

What's the best way to travel across the ocean? By sea turtle, of course! It was how Marlin and Dory traveled to Sydney, after all. Before they could say, "Rock out, dude," the traveling trio was cruising the California Current on their old friends, the sea turtles Crush and Squirt.

But getting to Morro Bay was just the beginning of Dory's search. How could you find someone if you didn't even remember their names?

As Dory and her friends left the California Current and swam through the shipping lanes into Morro Bay, they met some hermit crabs. Suddenly, Dory recalled that, once, when she was young, she had asked these hermit crabs if they knew where she could find "Jenny and Charlie." Jenny and Charlie! Those were her parents' names. She remembered them!

SEA TURTLE STATS 'N' FACTS

- As a species, sea turtles' evolution dates back at least 110 million years.

- There are seven species of sea turtles ranging from small to very, very large. One species, the leatherback sea turtle, can grow up to 1,000 pounds.

- Turtles sometimes look as if they are crying. But their tears are just helping them get rid of salt from the ocean water.

- Green sea turtles can stay underwater for up to five hours.

- Female sea turtles return to the same spot where they were hatched to lay their own eggs, even if that means traveling thousands of miles.

CRUSH & SQUIRT

The father-son duo of surfing sea turtle dudes who helped Dory and Marlin before are as friendly and easygoing as ever. They're always happy to help their friends get somewhere fast—especially if it means taking a really cool ride on a truly gnarly current. Hang onto your flippers, dude. It's Morro Bay or bust!

SQUIRT

"So long, Little Blue! Hope you find your parents!"

Into the Institute

The "Jewel of Morro Bay" turned out to be the "Marine Life Institute," a special facility where scientists rescue, rehabilitate, and release injured sea creatures back into the ocean. It is a beautiful place with many special exhibits where humans can learn more about the ocean environment and the creatures that live there.

As Marlin and Nemo watched, horrified, Dory was captured, tagged, and taken into the Institute. How were they ever going to get her out?

In the institute, Dory met a septopus —an octopus with seven arms—named Hank, who told her the tag meant she was going to be transferred to an aquarium in Cleveland. Dory didn't want to go, but Hank did. The solution? Dory would give Hank her transfer tag if he helped her find her family.

ALL ABOUT AQUARIUMS

Aquariums and scientific institutes like the Marine Life Institute provide many valuable services, such as:

- Making it possible to see ocean creatures you might never see in the wild.

- Researching and discovering information that helps save endangered species.

- Breeding threatened species to increase their survival rate.

- Inspiring humans to take care of ocean environments for the future.

Helping Arms

A solitary creature, Hank craves peace and quiet. All he wanted was to be transferred to the Marine Life Institute's more tranquil facility in Cleveland.

Hank can seem a little grumpy at times, but he has a heart of gold. When he agreed to lend Dory a helping tentacle—or seven—in exchange for her transport tag, Hank's cleverness, camouflage ability, and flexibility proved very useful. Although Hank said he just wanted to be alone, Dory's courage, optimism, and friendly ways won all three of his hearts.

"I don't like talking. I don't like chatter."

HANK

OUTSTANDING OCTOPUS FACTS

- Octopuses can change their color, skin pattern, and even skin texture in less than three-tenths of a second.

- When alarmed, an octopus will squirt a cloud of purple black ink and may swim away—at up to 25 miles per hour.

- Octopuses are considered one of the most intelligent of invertebrates (creatures with no backbone) and have been observed using tools such as coconut shells and rocks.

- There are approximately 240 suckers on each of an octopus's eight tentacles.

- An octopus has eight tentacles, three hearts, and no skeleton.

"I just want to live in a glass box alone. It's all I want! So give me your tag!"

Where's Hank?

Hank is a superstar at camouflage. He even makes himself look like:
- A cat poster
- White tile
- A black forklift
- Net
- Stair banister and pipes
- Brain coral
- Fake Dory hand puppet

MORE FRIENDS TO THE RESCUE

As Dory and Hank crept through the hallways of the Marine Life Institute, Dory spotted a picture of a purple shell on the map. It sparked another memory: She and her parents used to collect shells to make paths!

Meanwhile, Marlin and Nemo met two easygoing sea lions who knew how to get them into the Institute—in a bucket carried over the wall by a loon named Becky. Their plan didn't go as smoothly as they had hoped. Before they knew it, both Marlin and Nemo landed—*kersplash!*—in a fish tank in the Institute gift shop. Now what would they do?

FLUKE

RUDDER

FASCINATING SEA LIONS

- Sea lions evolved from bearlike ancestors millions of years ago.

- Sea lions can dive to depths of 1,000 feet and can hold their breath underwater for up to twenty minutes.

- Unlike seals, sea lions have external ear flaps. That's one of the ways you can tell them apart.

- Male sea lions can reach between 800 and 1,000 pounds and lengths of up to eight to nine feet.

FLUKE & RUDDER

Eat. Nap. Eat. Nap some more. Life is good when you have a nice sunny rock and plenty of fish, so why exert yourself? That's the philosophy of Fluke and Rudder, a pair of sea lions who used to live inside the Institute. Now they spend their days lazing around and keeping another sea lion named Gerald from lying on their rock. But when Marlin and Nemo ask for assistance, Fluke and Rudder agree to help. They know someone who can fly Marlin and Nemo into the Institute—a kooky, offbeat loon named Becky. There's only one problem: Becky can sometimes be a bit of a birdbrain!

A Voice from the Past

"We'd talk through the pipes when we were little. We were pipe pals!"

Still trying to find her parents, Dory landed in a tank with a whale shark named Destiny. To Dory's delight, she discovered that she and Destiny had once been "pipe pals" who spoke to each other through the pipes when Dory was growing up. In fact, that's how Dory learned to speak whale.

Dory wanted to get from Destiny's tank to the Open Ocean exhibit, but the only way was through some pipes, and she didn't like that idea at all. So the inventive and clever Dory came up with another plan: She would find her way across the MLI to the Open Ocean exhibit in a baby stroller. She just needed Hank to push her.

DESTINY

Rescued and brought to the Marine Life Institute at a young age, Destiny has very poor eyesight. It makes it hard for her to navigate, and she has very little confidence in her swimming ability. But when Destiny needs to help her long-lost pipe pal, Dory, a friendly beluga whale named Bailey guides Destiny and gives her the courage she needs to return to the ocean. That's the power of friendship!

WONDERFUL WHALE SHARKS

- Whale sharks can reach thirty feet in length (about the size of a school bus) and weigh 20,000 pounds (about the weight of two elephants).

- Whale sharks are filter feeders who eat plankton, algae, krill, and crab larvae.

- When whale sharks eat, they can open their mouths up to five feet wide—large enough to swallow a small bathtub.

- Whale sharks are known to be very calm and docile creatures.

- Every whale shark has a unique pattern of spots and stripes. No two are alike, much like human fingerprints.

TURN UP THE SOUND!

At last, Dory and Hank made it to the Open Ocean exhibit tank, and Hank gently put her in it. As Dory searched the tank for her parents, she followed a path of shells that led her to her childhood home.

But Dory's parents weren't there. Where were they now? Some friendly crabs told Dory that all the blue tangs had been taken to Quarantine and would be heading to Cleveland at the crack of dawn.

Dory had to reach them. But the only way to get to Quarantine was through the pipes. With her memory issues, Dory soon became lost. She called out to Destiny for help, and Destiny convinced Bailey to use his echolocation skills to guide Dory. To Bailey's amazement, it worked!

Meanwhile, Marlin and Nemo escaped the gift shop fish tank and reunited with Dory in the pipes. The three friends managed to find their way to Quarantine, where they met up with Hank again. Hank brought the three fish to the blue tang tank. They had to move fast before the truck left for Cleveland. Time was running out!

"I'm getting something! OOOooooOoo— here we go!"

BAILEY

Brought to the Marine Life Institute with a head injury, Bailey the beluga whale believed that his echolocation abilities were gone. Although the MLI doctors said Bailey was fine, the argumentative whale wouldn't even try to echolocate—until Dory needed his help. Then he came through loud and strong. It turned out that Bailey's troubles really were all in his head.

AMAZING BELUGA WHALE FACTS

- One of the most vocal whales in the ocean, beluga whales are sometimes known as "sea canaries."

- Beluga whales can change the shapes of their foreheads (called "melons") by blowing air into their sinuses.

- Beluga whales can actually swim backward.

From Tank to Truck to Ocean—Again!

When Dory finally reached the blue tang tank, she learned that her parents had come to Quarantine to look for her years ago. They weren't in the blue tang tank after all! Just then, the staff workers lifted the tank onto the truck. Dory had to get out!

Hank managed to scoop Dory into a glass beaker. But he couldn't get to Marlin and Nemo because they didn't swim into the cup. They were in the truck and on their way to Cleveland! Then a staffer spotted Hank and grabbed him. Hank lost his grip on the cup, and Dory fell to the floor and slipped down a drain marked DRAINS TO OCEAN. Dory ended up in the ocean, just outside the Marine Life Institute. She was lost and alone again.

For a moment, Dory panicked. Then she asked herself, "What would Dory do?" And just as she always did, Dory came up with a solution in her own special way. She swam into a kelp forest, and then spotted a trail of shells and followed them—straight to her parents. They had been waiting all this time for her to return. At last, Dory had found her family.

FASCINATING SEASHELLS!

- Seashells are actually the external skeletons of creatures known as mollusks.

- Scientists estimate that there are between 50,000 and 200,000 different varieties of mollusks in all the oceans of the world.

- All those beautiful colors and patterns on shells help the creatures inside stay hidden from predators. And the ridges and spines help protect them, too.

- The oldest known seashell collection was found in the ruins of the city of Pompeii, which was destroyed by a volcanic eruption in 79 AD.

FOLLOW THAT TRUCK!

Just then, Dory remembered her other family—Marlin and Nemo. Now they were on the truck to Cleveland. She had to get them off!

Using his echolocation skills, Bailey helped Destiny, Dory, and her parents follow the truck as it drove over a bridge across the bay. But Marlin and Nemo were still on the truck. Some very clever otters helped Dory get onto the truck so she could try to help Marlin and Nemo. Becky flew to the truck with a pail and got Marlin and Nemo out. But she forgot to bring Dory off the truck as well. Dory's adventures still weren't over!

SENSATIONAL SEA OTTERS

- Sea otters have the densest fur of any animal on Earth, with 850,000 to one million hairs per square inch of their bodies.

- Sea otters' fur keeps them warm and is essential to their well-being. So they clean it constantly.

- Sea otters are the only marine mammals that use tools such as rocks to break open shells for the food inside.

FREE IN THE SEA

It looked as if Dory's luck had run out. But she had another one of her amazing plans. In the ocean, Bailey's echolocation kept Dory's friends following close behind the truck.

Then, with some wild and crazy driving by Hank, the truck went off a cliff. As the truck flew toward the water, its doors popped open and the fish spilled out. Dory and Hank were free!

And Dory was finally reunited with her friends and family: her mother and father, Destiny, Bailey, Marlin, and Nemo.

EXTRA EXCITING ECHOLOCATION

- Whales and dolphins make high-frequency sounds and listen for the echoes to give them an "image" of their environment.

- "Echolocation" (e-ko-lo-ka-tion) is similar to the way your voice echoes in a big building. Whales use a series of fast clicks that sound like a continuous buzzing noise.

Friends and Family Forever

With help from Marlin, Nemo, and an ocean full of friends, Dory had done what she set out to do.

Back at the coral reef once again, Dory had never felt so happy. She had believed in herself and never stopped trying. Not only had she found her old family, but she had also discovered new friends and made them part of her family, too. It was wonderful to see them all together. Best of all, she remembered all their names!

MAKE IT YOUR OWN

Before you start building and decorating your model, read through the included instruction sheet so you understand how all the pieces come together. Then, choose a theme and make a plan. Do you want to make a replica of Dory as she appears in the films or try something different? Jellyfish, coral, seaweed—you could even dress Dory up in a Nemo costume. The options are endless! Here are some sample projects to get those creative juices flowing.

CLASSIC DORY

Dory in her natural blue tang state is always a winning look. Try your hand at this project to create a replica.

What You Need:
- Paintbrush
- White, magenta, blue, yellow, and black paint

What You Might Want:
- Green paint
- Bright blue paint
- ¼-inch Filbert paintbrush (This is a flat paintbrush with a rounded, oval edge that will make painting Dory's lines a little easier.)

PAINTING THE MODEL

1. Build your model up to step 11. Then paint the top and bottom fins blue.

2. Paint the tail yellow.

3. Outline the tail in black as shown and add a streak of black to the top edge of Dory's top fin.

4. Punch out the pieces that you need for the very next step. Paint these before putting them to the model. Follow the engravings on each piece so you know which should be painted what color. Once they are dry, add them to the model as directed.

5. Repeat step 4 for steps 12 to 40. You can work ahead if it helps, but be careful not to mix up the pieces!

Dory's Eyes

Paint the eyes white and let dry. Then paint a magenta circle in the middle. Finish by adding a smaller circle inside that for the pupils.

Dory's Stand

You can make the stand as simple or as elaborate as you like. For this example, a simple blue base to represent the ocean was used. The rest was painted green to resemble a seaweed patch.

29

Try adding a sequin or two to Dory's eyes for extra shine.

GLITTER PAINT

LOOSE GLITTER

GLITTER GLUE

GLITTERY DORY

There are several ways to make Dory bright and glittery. The example shown uses three different methods. Pick the one that works best for you.

Before adding any glitter, paint the model by following steps 1 through 5 of Classic Dory (page 28). Using a solid color as a base will always make the glitter brighter.

What You Need:
- Paintbrush
- White, magenta, blue, yellow, and black paint

What You Might Want:
- Glitter paint
- Glue and loose glitter
- Glitter glue
- Sequins

Glitter Method #1: Glitter Paint

This method is used for the black on Dory in the example.

1. Wait until the base coat paint dries.
2. Paint the glitter paint over the base.

TIP

You may have to do several coats of paint to get the glitter effect the way you want it. Make sure it's completely dry before switching colors.

Glitter Method #2: Glitter Glue

This method is used for the yellow on Dory in the example.

1. Make sure the base coat is completely dry.
2. Squeeze the glitter glue where you want it.
3. If you want a full coat of glitter, use an old paintbrush and spread it around the area you want it.

TIP

Glitter glue is very squishy and takes a while to dry. Make sure it sits in a place where nobody will touch it for twenty-four hours.

Glitter Method #3: Loose Glitter

This method is used for the blue on Dory in the example. Of all three methods, this is the messiest—but also the brightest and shiniest.

1. Using an old paintbrush or sponge brush, brush on a thin layer of glue where you want the glitter to go. Only do a patch of the area at a time so the glue doesn't dry out.
2. Sprinkle loose glitter over the layer of glue. Put more than you think you'll need so that there are no bare spots. Let sit for a minute or two.
3. Pick up the model and shake off the extra glitter into a trashcan or onto a piece of paper.
4. Repeat steps 1 through 3 until everything you want is covered in glitter.
5. Let the model dry completely.
6. To finish, take a dry paintbrush and gently brush off any loose glitter that may have fallen on another section.

For the stand:

This is an example of painting the coral reef that Dory lives in.

1. Paint the entire stand blue.
2. Paint coral shapes all over the stand in bright, vibrant colors.
3. To add more glitter, try one of the methods on this page.

IncrediBuilds™
A Division of Insight Editions LP, San Rafael, CA 94901
www.incredi-builds.com

Find us on Facebook: www.facebook.com/InsightEditions
Follow us on Twitter: @insighteditions

Library of Congress Cataloging-in-Publication Data available.

ISBN: 978-1-68298-001-9

Publisher: Raoul Goff
Acquisitions Manager: Robbie Schmidt
Art Director: Chrissy Kwasnik
Designer: Jenna Nybank
Executive Editor: Vanessa Lopez
Managing Editor: Molly Glover
Associate Editor: Katie DeSandro
Production Editor: Elaine Ou
Production Manager: Anna Wan
Craft and Instruction Development: Rebekah Piatte

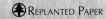

Insight Editions, in association with Roots of Peace, will plant two trees for each tree
used in the manufacturing of this book. Roots of Peace is an internationally renowned
humanitarian organization dedicated to eradicating land mines worldwide and
converting war-torn lands into productive farms and wildlife habitats. Roots of Peace
will plant two million fruit and nut trees in Afghanistan and provide farmers there with
the skills and support necessary for sustainable land use.

Manufactured in Shaoguan, China, by Insight Editions

10 9 8 7 6 5 4 3 2 1